The Real Poop
On the Dog Track

The Real Poop On the Dog Track

MICHAEL A. SISTI

OH!
ORSINI
HOUSE

The Real Poop on the Dog Track

Other books by Michael A. Sisti

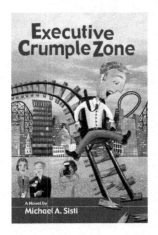

Orsini House, Sarasota, FL 34201
http://MichaelSisti.com

This book is dedicated to my social media family, my neighbors and my friends who constantly encourage me to entertain them with my twisted brand of humor.

Acknowledgements

This series of humor books contains a multitude of stories about my friends, neighbors and extended family. Many of you have provided me with countless opportunities to observe stuff that is almost always amusing and many times hilarious. This is a writer's treasure trove of material, so compiling these books was easy, not to mention fun. And in appreciation of the material you unsuspectingly presented, I decided to share the notoriety by using your real names whenever it seemed appropriate. In addition to the stories with a personal connection, there are many anecdotes gleaned from the unique lifestyles of living in New Jersey, Rhode Island and Florida.

In creating the covers for this series, I gave the assignment to Lea Orsini, a young illustrator and graphic designer who has an abundance of talent.

As usual, I had help getting from the rough drafts to finished manuscripts. I enlisted two of my trusted beta readers to review the text and provide input.

My British friend, Alan Nimmey, who now lives Bordeaux read the three books in this series and provided important edits. He was also a great sounding board, as he thoroughly enjoyed the humor.

My second reader was my wife Sara O. Sisti, who despite being familiar with most of the stories, blessed the effort while making her edits. Sara also made suggestions on the graphics for the text and cover.

Foreword–
How My Quirky Mind Works

If you read my recently published humor book, *Mosquitos, Snowbirds & Other Florida Pests,* you know how I developed the thought process to write stories like these. But if this is your first read of one of these books in the humor series, keep reading and learn how the twisted prism of my mind functions.

As far back as I can remember I have always tried to find a way to make the most boring, difficult, and painful tasks fun. This philosophy not only kept me sane and reasonably stress-free, but it also increased my enjoyment of life and gave me a strong appreciation of humor in our lives.

As I refined this process, I developed a keen sense of my surroundings and all the people I encountered. Watching their interactions and delving in their mindset opened a window that constantly feeds my imagination. I can take ordinary events and look at options and scenarios that make them even funnier than they already are.

When I was a school-age kid, I enjoyed telling jokes. It was fun to make people laugh. But then I started to tell stories about my family and about incidents that happened with my friends. And those anecdotes were even funnier than the jokes because they were real-life occurrences with real people.

During that stage of my development, I also discovered my penchant for creativity. As I combined my budding creative thinking with my observational skills, I began to ask 'what if?' whenever I encountered a humorous event. And that launched my writing career. I started adding humor to my classroom essays, papers, and letters, and then I began to write short stories. When I got into public speaking, my speeches and talks were sprinkled with my everyday experiences. And when email was introduced to the masses, I discovered a terrific new outlet to share my goofball ideas and thoughts. I found that the humor also kept people a little off balance. 'Did he really say that?' What did he actually want us to know with that story?'

In the late nineties, while we were living in Rhode Island, I was offered an opportunity to write an online column for a site that offered all kinds of information about The Ocean State. I called my column *Local Color* and my submissions were all about the unusual quirks of Rhode Island and its residents. Those submissions provided the basis for this humor book and it is named after one of the columns.

I have now written three novels, and they contain lots of emotion including anger and angst, but I soften the drama with humor, making for entertaining reading.

I hope you have as much fun reading my books as I had writing them (and living them).

Michael A. Sisti

Driving Directions

When I moved to Rhode Island in 1997, I found everything about the state and its people unusual, but nothing as strange as their quirky driving habits.

First, I learned that red lights are merely a suggestion to stop; and stop signs are only visible to drivers with out of state plates. There are also no street signs, except for some major arteries. So, try and figure out where you are when you enter a new neighborhood. I also learned that cars in Rhode Island don't come equipped with turn signals so you never know a driver's intentions. They feel their destination is their business and there's no need to share it with anyone. And speaking of sharing, if you're standing in a checkout line at the supermarket, the person in front of you, without prompting, will tell you her most intimate secrets, and with much more graphic information than you really need or are comfortable receiving.

Another is the license plate thing. A low numbered plate is worth more than a pound of gold in this state. When you think about it, all it means is that someone in your family knows a politician. So big deal! In the first three years I lived there, I met four governors, even played golf with one of them and his wife, and my license number is a standard issue, and has three digits, high ones at that. And my plate doesn't have one of those state police emblems on it that's supposed to make you exempt from getting traffic tickets.

Speaking of traffic tickets, what ever happened with the traffic court 'scandal'. I had read that something like $25 million in fines went uncollected. That's more money than most Rhode Island companies earn in their lifetime. But according to recent articles, the state will recover all the money. They sent letters out to the scofflaws telling them to pay their fines or they would lose their low numbered plates. And worse, the potholes on their street would not be filled. The problem is, the court doesn't really know who owes the money, so all the collection letters were sent to 'Current Occupant'.

The first time I came to Providence I saw this billboard on I95 and the headline read, 'Dare to Cross the Bridge?' It was an advertisement for a car dealer in East Providence. Not being familiar with the vernacular, I asked the people at the company where I was consulting to explain its meaning. I had assumed that the bridge to East Providence was in danger of imminent collapse; or that snipers were shooting from high-rise buildings at drivers crossing the bridge. Well, it was explained to me that west bay residents would never consider driving to the east bay to buy a car, even if they could save thousands of dollars. And east bay residents feel the same way. I said, 'But East Providence can't be more than ten minutes from that billboard. Surely people would drive that far to save a couple a grand.' I was wrong, however. Apparently, it's like going to a foreign country. People will drive any reasonable distance on their side of the line, but they won't cross it. They think they may need their passport.

And then my new friends laid the big one on me. They told me that people in Woonsocket have never been outside the town (or is it city?) not even to visit Providence, which I later learned is only 15 miles away. I said, 'Where's Woonsocket?' They replied, 'Oh, it's faa.'

So, I looked it up on a map and it's only twenty minutes from downtown. I jumped in my car and drove up there. After commuting three hours to get to Providence from New Jersey, a twenty-minute hop to Woonsocket is like going out for a newspaper. Well, I got

4

into Woonsocket and I found that people there have cars, and there are gas stations, so transportation is not an issue. Eventually, I found my way out of town and back to Providence, and it was easy. Even the movie-producer duo, the Farrelly brothers who were born in Woonsocket found their way out.

So, what's with the Woonsocketonians? Why won't they leave their quaint city? What do they know that we don't?

Red Light District

In a desperate move to raise even more revenue, many cities and towns in the Ocean State are targeting traffic violators. The idea was spawned by the release of the national study of driving habits, which is conducted annually. It revealed that Rhode Islanders have the worst driving records in the country. Once again, the state came in dead last. No pun intended.

But a more important statistic in a local study on traffic violations has caught the attention of budget directors everywhere. The report from that study revealed that video cameras placed in random locations for a total of about 8,600 hours, equivalent to one year's time, recorded nearly 1,400 drivers who ran red lights. For each traffic light, that amounts to about six and a half violations an hour. (Is it half a violation when someone drives into the intersection against the light, and then backs up?)

Next consider that Rhode Island has more traffic lights per square mile than other states. Multiply every traffic light by 1,400 and then by $150 for each fine, plus court costs. We now have the ingredients for the perfect storm for traffic fine collection. If there was a way to ticket all these offenders, the state could almost certainly do away with property taxes entirely and concentrate on red light runners. This potential has budget managers throughout the state salivating all over their spreadsheets.

When the politicians at the State House heard about this potential windfall, they began to look for ways to spend the extra money rather than reduce other taxes in the state. In anticipation, they started preparing bills to be enacted that would provide automobiles for each legislator, paid for by the State, expense accounts at the

Capital Grill for the governor, his executive staff and all state senators and representatives, and paid golf memberships for elected state officials and cabinet members. All this even before the red light program was approved.

The problem that emerges is how do you catch these offenders? We can't put a police officer on every corner. Installing video cameras is a solution, but there's a catch there – the cost. These cameras with electronic sensors run $30,000 to $70,000 each, plus the expense of the union electricians installing them all over the state. It would take years to recoup that kind of investment, and by then there would be other budget shortfalls to fund. The cities, towns and municipalities need money now.

Well one enterprising city manager came up with a creative solution. In fact, he got the idea from a recent column on text messaging. He began hiring teenagers to stand on every street corner and take pictures of violators with their camera phones. They would then key in the license number of the vehicle, the time, date and location, plus a description of the driver and car. Because of the special skills of these young people, this can be done in a matter of seconds. Instead of paying these kids, they would be rewarded with steady supplies of I-Tunes and video games. The ancillary benefit of using teenagers for this solution is that the ACLU and other extreme left-wing fringe groups cannot label this a 'Big Brother' activity. Some people however, might argue that the local governments are exploiting child labor. And of course, the unions will want to organize them.

But the story doesn't end there, as it looks like Yankee ingenuity just may prevail. The website, ReallyScaryMasks.com, having just completed its Halloween shipments to stores around the country, has come up with a way to help the traffic violators, and extend their business from seasonal to year round. They have created masks of all the local politicians and are marketing them to the offending drivers to wear when they drive, particularly if they run a light. It's a brilliant idea because everyone knows the pols in Rhode Island have diplomatic immunity.

Who Moved My Salami

I read this book a while back that was all the rage. It was called Who Moved My Cheese? All the bureaucrats in my company were so infatuated with its seemingly breakthrough content, that they were making the book required reading within their departments. But before I forced my team to read it, I wanted to make sure it was worth their time.

The book was about this mouse that got his whiskers bunched up because someone moved his cheese to another spot. When the mouse couldn't find his cheese in the usual place, he became confused, paranoid and angry. He just couldn't adjust to the fact that he would have to look elsewhere to find his cheese. As I read the book, I concluded that this mouse was dumber than dirt. When I finished the book, I yawned and threw the book in the trash, feeling that I had been taken in by all the hype about this novel approach to dealing with change.

Being a lover of food, however, the book gave me pause when I thought about what would occur if something like this were to happen to people. Say, for instance you went into a supermarket and the robbies were now in the pet food section. (For those of you unfamiliar with 'robbies', it is broccoli rabe, a somewhat bitter cousin to broccoli.) Although I enjoy broccoli rabe often, I had never heard it called 'robbies' before moving to Rhode Island. I guess it is part of the local vernacular. It's in the same category as cabinets (coffee milk shakes) and stuffies (stuffed clams), two other words that I would never have expected to find on a restaurant menu.

How would you react if you ordered a pepperoni pizza from Domino's and the pepperoni came thin sliced in a little plastic tube, just like Pringle's potato chips? And speaking of that, did you ever wonder where they find enough potatoes exactly same size to make those chips?

Where would you be if they moved all the Dunkin' Donuts shops? You drive to your favorite shop and find it's been moved to the top floor of a six-story walk-up. And what's with all the donut shops in Rhode Island anyway? With Dunkin' Donuts, Honey Dew, Bess Eaton, Allie's and now Krispy Kremes, we have more donut shops per capita than any other state in the country. I heard the new governor is going to add that fact to the sign down on I 95 when you cross the border from Connecticut. It will read something like this, 'Rhode Island, where you're never more than 100 feet from a donut shop.' And it's being sponsored by Ocean State Cardiology Associates.

To me the most traumatic move would be if they took all the garlic out of the food stores and sold it only in Benny's Appliances. Fortunately, this would never happen, because it would be a logistical nightmare to move that much stuff. Ever since I moved to Rhode Island, I was convinced that the largest company in the state was the garlic distributor in Providence.

Next time you go to Federal Hill and pick up a dry salami off the counter in Venda Ravioli, think about how easy it was, and how you didn't have to get all stressed out finding a dry cleaner that sold it.

So, there you go. Now you don't have to read the book.

A Pain in the Ass

I'm a nervous wreck as I am about to have a prostate biopsy taken, this the third one in my short time on this planet. I got an urgent call from my urologist's office, scheduling an appointment for the test. Most men aren't familiar with the process. So, here's the inside scoop on how it works.

First, as I'm sitting in the exam room in my tighty-whities, Nurse Hardasse comes in and greets me with her usual, 'Hi Big Guy.' Then she starts to giggle. I hate when she does that. It makes me feel so inadequate. She then tells me to lie on the examining table on my side facing the wall, in a partial fetal position. Once there, she raises the table to a height that almost allows me to touch the ceiling, explaining that the doc likes to work standing upright. She hands me one of those useless paper wraps that slide off with your first move, and as she leaves the room tells me to put on the sheet and remove my shorts.

I lay the wrap over my bare body, and as I go to pull off the shorts, as expected, the sheet falls to the floor. I look down at the crumpled mess in panic. There's no way I'm jumping off the table to retrieve it. Even if I don't break a leg, I'll never be able to climb back up. So, lying there with all this anxious energy, I take off my shorts and toss them to the chair that is stacked with my other clothes. My exuberant toss from this height causes them to hit the rotating ceiling fan and they get hung up on one of the revolving blades. With both of these problems out of my control, I lay back down on the gurney and face the wall.

As Doctor Goldfinger, the male gynecologist, and his team, come into the room, they are greeted by my blushing bare cheeks, et al. Ms. Hardasse looks around and says, 'Hey Big Guy did we miss the keg party?' Giggle, giggle. She then introduces me to her assistant, Crisco Galore, who begins to lubricate my butt with axle grease and inserts a high definition studio camera in a place where you never thought it would fit. Since I am facing the wall with a strategically placed TV monitor mounted on it, I now see the screen come alive and I'm looking at the inside of Carlsbad Caverns.

At that point, Dr. Strangeglove wedges a Daisy BB rifle into the orifice and begins firing away. OK, so maybe it was only a cap pistol, but it stung like a BB gun. He shot 21 needles into my highly sensitive, albeit numbed prostate. During this assault, I felt a warm liquid oozing onto my thigh. Looking down I saw a small pool of blood. Becoming alarmed, I feared that one of the needles had gone clear through my boys, causing permanent damage to my male reproductive equipment. Fortunately, it turned out to be just some of last night's red wine that had leaked out. And now I understood why you should never drink alcohol before any medical procedure. And finally, after all this uncomfortable, dignity-deflating activity, I heard the latex gloves snap, and I knew I had survived the ordeal.

Well, today I'm back in my urologist's office to get the results of the torture test. He gave me the good news that all the tissue samples were clear, except for the gunpowder burns. And the good doctor explained that at least for the time being, I won't require a permanent Viagra/Flomax/Depends dependency. And that's better than a kick in the ass.

But, like you I wonder, with all the negative indicators and no sign of cancer, what is wrong with my prostate? Self-diagnosing my problem, I'm convinced it is either virus or bacteria borne. And to prove my theory, I'm sitting here naked, half turned to watch my butt in a mirror, waiting for it to sneeze.

Reach Out and Touch Someone

Have you called your phone company lately? It's a truly emotional experience, similar to talking to Support Services at your Internet provider.

I'm simply trying to temporarily transfer my cell phone number to the global phone I'm taking to Europe. So I dial the carrier 1-800-EXASPERATE and I get the usual mechanical voice prompts: 'Please listen carefully as our options have been downgraded.' Dial one for English, two for Spanish, three for Swahili . . . All others remain on the line.' 'In order to serve you better please enter your 10-digit phone number followed by the pound sign. What is your date of birth? What is your mother's maiden name? In what city were you born? Please wait while I retrieve your records.' (time passes) 'All of our representatives are busy helping other helpless victims, so please hold on and your call will be answered in the order it was received. We can't give you an estimated time because we're still assisting extremely dense people that called three days ago.' (More time passes)

The elevator music stops and I think someone is going to pick up, but instead I get a recorded message. 'Did you know that your telecommunications carrier has just been acquired by the Pullet Pellet Company making us the world's largest communications and manure company?' (I'm thinking: Are they now going to compete with the Federal Government? Much more time passes and I'm starting to get antsy.)

'Hell-ou, I am helping you. My name is Dillip.'

'Hi Phillip. I have a simple . . .'

'No, no sir, it is Dillip, not Phillip. For security purposes, can you give me your 10-digit telephone number, your date of birth, your mother's maiden . . .'

'Hang on Phillip, Dillip, Dollop, or whatever the frig your name is. I gave that information at the beginning of the call early this morning.'

'Oh, sir, that's impossible, it's not morning yet.' (That's when I realized that I was talking to someone in Bombay.)

'Look, Dillip, all I want to do is transfer my cell number to this global phone.'

'This is also too bad sir, but I cannot be helping you with this matter. Please hold the line and I will transfer to you the correct department.' (More time passes, so I start making lunch with the phone on speaker mode.)

'This is Imelda, how can I be of service?'

'I guess Dipshit, I mean Dillip didn't explain that I'm trying to transfer my cell number to a global phone.'

'Oh no darling. I cannot be of help to you. I will get someone to assist you immediately.' (Endlessly more time passes, while I make an afternoon snack reciting 'Serenity Now, Serenity Now.')

'Good morning to you, this is Mr. Galani from the Global Phone Service Department. May I be of service?' (Home at last. I feel relieved.)

'Hi Mr. G. How's the weather in the Philippines?'

'Actually sir, I am in Pakistan. But now before I can assist you, please give me the 10-digit telephone number, your date of birth . . .'

'Whoa, there Galani. I gave that friggin' information out three times and there's no damn way I'm doing it again. You figure it out. Better yet, get your supervisor on the line. And make it fast. I've been on-hold so long I need another shower.' (Lots more time elapses, so I start searching the medicine cabinet for the Valium.)

'Hello sir, this is Mr. Mamood, the supervising director on the line with Mr. Galani. What is the problem with you providing your 10-digit number and the other information?'

'Aaaagh! Do you people have any idea what you've put me through today? I am going insane. You are so smug and polite, and now you have me so crazed, I'm getting suicidal.'

When they heard that, they got very excited, and Mamood said, 'Suicidal? Sir, can you drive a truck?'

Low Blow from the High Court

The Supreme Court decision striking down medical marijuana use is a tragedy for America's suffering masses. Reaction to the ruling was swift, vocal and strong. Lotus Windsong, President of the California-based *High Sierra*, and Ecstasy Blossoms, founder of *D.O.P.E.* (Doing Opiates Promotes Eroticism), in a joint statement angrily responded, 'What are these judges smoking? Don't they know that millions of very sick people will no longer be able to get their *prescription* filled at the local head shop? It's going to drive them back to the schoolyards to find their medication.' Dr. Les Payne, who runs a chain of pharmacy and medical appliance stores, called *Bongs and Blows*, observed, 'A dark cloud has come over the sick and indigent in this country. My patients are in a state of abject fear scrambling to find a substitute medication. They're futilely trying to mix combinations of oregano, basil, St. John's Wort and other substances to find the next cure.'

The medicinal benefits of marijuana have been documented in countless cases, as people with a plethora of illnesses have come forth to describe their miracle cures. Some of these afflictions are extremely rare and obscure, with no known treatment.

Willy Chouque, who was diagnosed with an extreme case of agitatus nervousum, feels he can't survive without his medical-strength weed. In his induced state, he became a spokesperson for the benefits of marijuana. Now, without his medication, his condition prevents him from even discussing his affliction in public. So he sits in his room with the shades drawn and the lights dimmed. And he is just one of the many faces that have been forced to recede into the shadows, smoldering in obscurity.

Anorexia sufferers have found that usage of the drug helps them regain their appetites. This may explain why marijuana treatment is so popular in Hollywood. The trickle-down effect of the ruling however, will soon impact the entire food service industry. Sources at Krispy Kreme expressed concern over the situation. They feel that with marijuana usage abruptly ceasing, patients will no longer have the urge to rush down to the donut shop for a 'fix'. They are planning large layoffs and curtailing contracts for flour and sugar. For its part, Dunkin Donuts has scrapped plans for the introduction of its new Brainscramble Brownies, available by prescription only.

In Mexico, where the roach is the national pet, the government is furious with the US high court ruling and is threatening to close its borders. As part of the NAFTA agreement, Mexico's national pharmaceutical manufacturer, Hallucinata Groupo, had been in full production of millions of nickel bags of marijuana that were carried over the border by undocumented migrant workers. Mexico's president, Vincente Fox, who himself is dependent on this life-saving medication, blamed the whole incident on President Bush, calling it a vast right-wing conspiracy (a phrase he shamelessly hijacked from the Clintons). In fact, Fox had taken his prescription just before his speech about black American workers. Immediately following the speech, Rev. Al Sharpton flew to Mexico City to meet with Fox, and learn first-hand about the medicinal benefits of this wonder drug. And after smoking placebos all these years, the Reverend has experienced the real deal. And he's now convinced that he will be the next president.

But for pain sufferers everywhere, there is a glimmer of hope. One of the Internet Blogs just reported that coke will soon be back in Coca-Cola, giving new meaning to 'It's the Real Thing!' In the meantime, everyone is socking away poppy seeds in anticipation of the next blockbuster decision by the high courts. And those chronic patients, who still have a stash, are toking it to the limit.

Talk is Cheap

When I was a teenager, tooling around in my Chevy that ran on twenty-five cents a gallon gas, the car radio constantly blasted rock and roll music. Whoever 'rode shotgun' in the car (front passenger seat) was in charge of the radio. Whenever an announcer came on for a commercial, news or other break, we changed the station. It was non-stop Elvis, Bill Haley and the Big Bopper.

But while rock (or rap) still rules with the younger generation, and car radios play even louder, adults have switched to talk radio. Rush Limbaugh, the godfather of radio talk shows, hit a hot button when he offered an alternative to the so-called 'elite media'. He blathered on for two hours or more preaching conservatism and jousted with callers who challenged his views. This was in stark contrast to the liberal diatribe served up by the big three TV networks, CNN and the major newspapers. Limbaugh's message resonated with consumers and soon there were several other nationally syndicated hosts on the air, including Hannity, Medved, Coulter and others. Add the hundreds of local talk-show hosts that took to the airwaves around the country and you had a revolution in radio broadcasting. Finding a niche between the liberal elite media and the conservative talk shows was Fox News, with their slogan, *Fair and Balanced Reporting.* They presented both sides of an issue and let the viewer decide. This format enables you to think about an issue and draw your own conclusions, although most people still want someone else to do their thinking for them.

The talk show medium became so strong and influential that it impacted elections and helped swing the power in government from liberal to conservative (except in California and Rhode Island among others, of course). So the liberals, not acknowledging their control of the elite media cried foul. Talk radio was unfairly attacking liberalism. And so they countered with their own version of talk radio and pumped millions into the liberal flagship talk radio show, *Air America.*

I listened to it on a local station once, and rather than stimulate me, I found myself dozing at the wheel. This had to be the most boring fare I've ever heard on radio. While I lean moderately conservative, I share many liberal views, and I like hearing all sides of an argument. However, this wasn't a factual presentation of liberal philosophy, it was mindless drivel, sprinkled with long pauses of silence (a deadly characteristic for radio). With the major newspapers losing huge chunks of subscribers and TV networks like CBS crumbling, the liberals better come up with something better than *Air America*, if they hope to level the playing field.

Locally, Cranston Mayor Stephen Laffey has his own radio show, and it must be touching a liberal nerve. Recently, a complaint was filed with the Board of Elections to get him off the air. The charge is that he's using the show to get re-elected. From my perspective, anyone that would spend two hours a week on the air, plus another few hours preparing for the show, just to be re-elected mayor of Cranston deserves the job. The courts, however have ruled that airing his show is a violation of the election laws, and he is not protected by first amendment rights. The decision is being appealed, so we won't know the final outcome for some time to come, probably after the elections are over. Stay tuned!

Smoked Out

Now that Rhode Islanders have gotten a whiff of the new smoking ban, most of them are pleased with it. But the smoking class is not happy. You would think the Legislature, in its infinite wisdom, would have started the ban in the summer instead of the dead of winter. Get people used to smoking outdoors when the weather is nice, rather than break them in during a blizzard. In Florida the ban is much more stringent. You can't smoke in any indoor facility where people are employed. This is just about everywhere but your home. On the coldest winter day however, the temperature is forty degrees, so smokers don't mind stepping out to light up.

When I was a kid, people smoked everywhere: on the job, in their cars and homes, at every public function and in every public place. But those smokers are gone now. They all died of lung cancer. Back then, my father, uncles and older cousins all hung out at a local bar where they smoked constantly, and drank beer. I guess we were an untraditional Italian family. None of us drank wine, but everyone consumed beer, and lots of it. I remember when the rumor spread around the bar's patrons that the owner was going to ban smoking at the bar. He was developing some kind of breathing disorder. My father immediately ordered a tank car of Schlitz Premium delivered to the house. Although my mother didn't allow smoking in the living quarters, the men began hanging out in our finished basement, playing billiards on our new pool table, drinking beer and smoking. After a while, the white drop ceiling, which was probably made of asbestos, turned brown, the dog died, the cat ran away, and the smell of smoke remained forever. But we never saw another insect or mouse in our basement.

I was one of the fortunate few who never got hooked on smoking. My father convinced me not to smoke and I never did. The indoctrination started when I was five. Sitting at a table with the adults at a family function, I picked his freshly lit cigarette out of the ashtray and tried to take a puff. He stopped me and said, 'If you're going to smoke, you should first find out what it tastes like.' He then stubbed out the cigarette and made me eat it. That was a culinary experience I will never forget. Later, when I was twelve, he took all the joy out of my teen-age years when he gave me permission to smoke. Imagine that! He told me that I could smoke anytime, anywhere, except in the house, and he would supply the smokes. How could you be a rebellious kid when you could light up and not be disobeying your parents? Without the lure of getting caught, smoking was kind of boring, so I didn't get hooked.

I understand that for some of you smokers, this indoor smoking ban is a serious blow to your civil liberties. Sitting at my computer in my office in Sarasota Florida, I can hear you shouting all the way from Providence that your God-given right to smoke wherever you want is being trampled. But perhaps this ban will cause you to smoke one less cigarette today, and allow you to breathe the fresh air for one more day. I'm only 77, but I have already been breathing fresh air for over 11,300 more days than my father did.

Instead of venting against this smoking ban, why don't you channel all that rage against something serious, like the taxes in Rhode Island?

Pardon My French

With all due respect to Rhode Islanders of French ancestry, I am having a growing problem with the people of France. And they don't seem to like me. Actually, it's not me personally, but all Americans and everything American that they despise. Are they jealous of our success or do they really think they are so much more superior? I just don't get it.

I remember when Euro-Disney opened in France (a location that Eisner later realized was a major mistake) the French people boycotted it because it was too *American*. In an effort to prevent our culture from contaminating theirs, the French government limits the distribution of American-made movies, music and other entertainment. Do they really consider their culture that fragile? Can you picture a sniveling, snooty, aristocratic Frenchman becoming a grunge-wearing, hip-hopping rapper, drinking Colt 45 from a can?

There was a time when France was a world power. They came to the aid of the American colonists and helped us defeat England to win our independence. But after two hundred years of socialist stagnation, and two world wars, their strength diminished dramatically and they now wield very little influence in the international arena. Their one remaining power is their veto on the UN Security Council, a weapon that they wield ad nauseum. While once a military powerhouse, they now make beautiful uniforms for other armies. When I went to school, I was encouraged to study French as that was deemed to be the preferred language of international commerce, science and diplomacy. Now, around the world, everyone is learning English, as that has become the language of choice. That must really grate their fromage. Another possible reason for the rift involves the rumor surrounding the gift from France of the Statue of Liberty. The year we received it, we were not doing too well financially. So, that Christmas, we reciprocated by sending them 200 cases of barbecued ribs and a thousand pounds of grits. But that was over a hundred years ago. They should have gotten over it by now.

Why do the French dislike us so much? And will our retaliation cause a permanent chasm between our two countries? I'm convinced that their arrogance and rigidity is the result of severe constipation from their diet of overly rich foods. All that paté, cheese and escargot would sure bind me up pretty tight. For their part, the French think we are over-medicated, spoiled, overweight, pampered peasants with a serious lack the sophistication to appreciate life's finer pleasures.

Otherwise we would eat nothing but French cuisine. And drink only French wine at three meals a day. I just happen to like American food, particularly when it is fused with Asian, Italian, Hispanic and even French influences. They don't know what they are missing. And I love American wines, as well as Australian, Chilean, and South African, among others. In France, they're still washing their cars with California wines.

The news media in France never misses a chance to blast American imperialism. Their courts hammer US companies, and French people are deliberately rude to tourists from America. But beneath the façade, they are watching bootleg American movies, pirating our music on the Internet, and eating Monsieur Mac's All Boeff Pattes, le Grande Coke, et Pommes de Fries France avec Catsuppe.

Dark Clouds and
Silver Linings

Over the summer, a traveling show from Oregon made its way to Providence to expose Rhode Islanders to the world of spirits and 'allow them to touch what's untouchable'. The recent weekend event featured tarot card readers, psychics, healers, palm readers, gypsies and fakirs (or were they fakers?), exhibiting their wares and their assorted talents. One of the most interesting exhibits was a setting where for a mere $25 you could get your photo taken. Of course, your photo wasn't taken with any ordinary camera. This special camera, purported to cost $9,700 is capable of photographing your aura.

When I saw this demonstration, I became intrigued by the possibilities. The young woman who had just been photographed, was showing everyone her picture with this bright yellow haze surrounding her head and shoulders. The photographer, fakir or whatever he was, explained that the yellow glow signified a sunny personality. Other explanations included the theory that the light was from angels surrounding the subject and giving off this energy.

I liked that theory, and it got me thinking. What if we had used one of these cameras during the presidential election campaign? We could have been saved from being bombarded by billions of dollars in negative advertising, and we wouldn't have had to stay up and watch those boring debates. We could have simply taken pictures of Trump and Clinton and saw who had the best aura. You can't fake an aura, can you? Both of their smiles are genuine, and I'm sure a big smile contributes to a bright, sunny glow. What are the possibilities that they both had dark, cloudy auras?

Looking for ways to capitalize on this new technology, I came up with an idea to test the accuracy of this marvelous gift of science. I contacted the authorities to get permission to go to the nearest adult correctional facility and photograph the auras of the inmates who were convicted of the most heinous crimes. I would then go to the capitol and photograph the local politicians. You know, the ones who won by landslides, or ran unopposed. I expected that the photo comparison between the two groups of incarcerated and elected inmates would be fascinating. But then again, you might not be able to tell one from the other.

Well, the upstanding leaders of our fine state were having none of this. Not only did my permission request get denied but they went as far as trying to revoke my driver's license, voter registration, library card and even my Stop & Shop discount card. These guys play hardball.

Still fascinated by the possibility of seeing someone's aura, I decided to purchase one of these $9,700 marvels. I went on the Internet and actually located the source. I found the Aura Camera for the unbelievable price of only $749. That's about $9,000 less than the list price. I later found one on ebay for $250. And it included everything you need to go into the aura business. It came with all the accessories, including a full color poster to hang in front of your parlor to attract those gullible customers. I didn't read all of the literature, but I'm sure the kit came with a full set of stock auras, in all the latest colors, and a tiny broom to clean up the angel dust.

Save the Earth

One of the most feared organizations in the minds of Rhode Islanders is not al Qaida or the Islamic State (ISIS). It's the Department of Environmental Management (DEM). If you are planning to do anything to your private property in Rhode Island, even planting a tree, you are at the mercy of the DEM. Unless of course, you are a politician. Then you can even drain a reservoir without fear of reprisal. But us regular Joes cringe in the shadow of their far-overreaching jurisdiction.

A few years ago, I produced a plan to develop a golf course community on several hundred acres in the southern part of the state. Now in my mind, this was an excellent use of the land in question. It would result in the retention of hundreds of acres of open space, providing sanctuary for birds and wildlife. It would also dramatically limit the density of housing in the area. And it would provide abundant outdoor recreation and appreciation of nature for tens of thousands of people. However, some tree-hugging, dung-collecting, sap-sniffing, centipede-studying environmentalist just happened to discover a rare species of the Salivating Marsh Crite on the property. It seems that this survivor of the Jurassic Age had found peace and tranquility in only one small habitat in the entire world. And its location turned out to be on an overgrown, abandoned farm in Hopkinton. Since there would be a miniscule possibility of disturbing the 10-year cycle of the mating ritual of this critical member of the food chain (they live to create havoc in flower and vegetable gardens) there would be no golf course.

And the problem is not just in Rhode Island. Out on the Left Coast, the environmentalists are having a field day with their new auto emissions mandate. This new rule would cut, not poisonous carbon monoxide, but carbon dioxide by 30% within the next several years. This is the stuff you exhale and is vital to the survival of all plants and trees. Not only will this effort reduce the carbon dioxide level by a barely measurable one-twentieth of one percent, it will add an incredible $3,000 to the cost of every car. And for what reason? Are shrubs and bushes getting high on too much carbon dioxide? Is there a looming obesity epidemic among trees? Are they growing so high that they are endangering low-flying aircraft? Makes you wonder.

As it turns out, environmental regulations are not meant for environmentalists. They have been put in place to keep law-abiding citizens in place. And here's an example of how those regulations protect our environment by keeping us in line, while the enviro-special interests totally ignore the law.

Recently the Arctic Sunrise, a boat owned by Greenpeace (the radical mother of all environmental groups) recently entered Alaskan waters without the required oil spill prevention plan, or proof of financial responsibility should a spill occur (The Green Geek Lobby pressured the EPA for this far overreaching mandate). The vessel, which carries 128,000 gallons of fuel and lubricants was in Alaska protesting logging activities. They weren't protesting oil drilling, but logging. Now there's a noble cause. Where would we be without wood, one of the few renewable resources on the planet?

When the environmental group was notified of the violations, they agreed as ordered to remain anchored until the situation was remedied. Instead, the Arctic Sunrise left port that very morning and went sailing right into critical 'environmentally sensitive' areas during peak salmon runs, without care or consideration for the potential catastrophic impact.

A lawyer for Greenpeace was quoted as saying that these onerous environmental regulations are 'getting to be far too complicated in this day and age.' Think about that the next time you want to put a decorative footbridge over the babbling brook that runs through your property. Or is it their property?

Don't Let the Bedbugs Bite

Just in case you needed something else to keep you awake at night, there are reports that Rhode Island is among the growing number of states that have been found to have bedbug infestations. This is not a joke. In fact, it brings new meaning to the term 'Blood-sucker'.

In a recent interview with a spokesperson from the company purported to be the largest bug control company in the state (at least they have the largest bug on display), Tony 'The Swat' Macaluso couldn't hide his elation when he declared, 'Bedbug eradication is a growth industry.' Makes you wonder just how big these tiny creatures can get. He predicts that you will soon find bedbugs in movie theaters, subways and airports. After hearing that, I relaxed a bit. After all, there are no subways in Rhode Island, and I don't sleep in theaters and airports.

He went on to say that they can also be found in some of the most exclusive hotels (these days, with a credit card, even a homeless person can get in almost anywhere) and are extremely prevalent in college dormitories. It seems that the little buggers like the exotic chemicals found in students' blood. The bugs are tiny, about one-quarter inch in diameter, and they like to hide side by each, between floorboards and creases in mattresses. They puncture your skin with three holes (breakfast, lunch and dinner) and suck out several times their weight in blood. And contrary to rumor, this does not lower your blood pressure.

News reports claim that the incidence of bedbug infestation has increased 70 percent each year since 2000 when there was a 300 percent jump in documented infestations. And there is no letup in sight. This situation has vampires alarmed, as this is rapidly becoming a serious threat to their territory. They have hired a lobbyist to petition the Rhode Island Legislature to pass a law forcing the bedbugs to become unionized and follow work rules.

Unfortunately, effective bedbug eradication is practically impossible. Politically correct and environmentally friendly mandates have removed the option of pesticide spraying for the bugs, so they keep multiplying and spreading. At this rate, a good night's sleep is going to become a rarity. The best way to protect yourself at bedtime is to wrap your body in Saran Wrap and cover your face with molasses. (The molasses acts like fly paper.) This way you can sleep tight and the bedbugs won't bite.

Mad Deer Disease

I'm sure I told you about the deer problems I've had over the years and how they eat all our vegetables, flowers, and shrubs. As you know I've spent years in a losing battle against these agile, voracious creatures, without success. One of my mottos is, 'If you can't beat them, join them. And then beat them.' And that's what we did. We couldn't scare them away, so we decided to attract more of them.

And that's how we finally figured how to take advantage of these freeloaders who consume thousands of dollars-worth of plantings a year. We've started deer farming. It's a terrific new business. In fact, anyone living on a half-acre tract or more is considering it. Every town's zoning department is being flooded with variance requests to change to farming, so homeowners can lower their property taxes. A guy in Washington, DC got turned down, however. He wanted to raise a herd on the National Mall.

After all that Mad Cow stuff in the papers, people are afraid of eating beef, so there's a real demand for venison. And just about every state is overrun with deer. All you have to do is keep planting all those flowers and shrubs that they love to eat. They will show up with their friends and family, and that's how you fatten them up. When they look like the overstuffed pigs that they are, you give them this special anesthesia that numbs them up. Then you stick them in the back of the SUV and run them down to the butcher. Venison is much leaner than beef and it's great for people on the South Beach diet.

Oh, and there's also a great by-product, antlers. You cut off the antlers and grind them up into this powder, which sell for a couple of hundred dollars a pound. The powder has medicinal properties. Ancient Eastern medicine practitioners claim it has healing power and can prevent cancer. Of course, there are the aphrodisiac powers that the powder is also rumored to possess. And it's probably true. Just look at the explosion of deer running around the place. They had to come from somewhere.

The other by-product is the pellets that they make every day. What you do is save them up for a year, and when the local golf course aerates its fairways, you sell the pellets to the club as fertilizer to fill in the holes.

If you are serious about starting your own deer herd, you have to be aware of one thing. Deer can get Mad Deer Disease, just like cows. It's actually not called that however. It's called Chronic Wasting Disease. I once worked for a company that had an epidemic of it. They must have been serving portions of the tainted venison in the company cafeteria. Within a week, the restroom toilets were clogging and all the workers started calling in sick. But when their the septic tanks in their yards began backing up, they started buying tickets to the sport venues, just to use the public restrooms.

Crossing Guards
Go to School

For Rhode Islanders out of work or looking for a career change, here is an opportunity you can't afford to miss. Why not consider the school crossing guard profession? Starting salaries are a whopping $45 per hour and compensation includes 100% covered health insurance benefits, paid vacation the entire summer, pension and retirement benefits, uniform allowance and more. That's just under what plastic surgeons and pizzeria owners make. And you'll get to join a really prestigious union. I think it's the same one that the independent home daycare providers belong to. Still not convinced? Consider this. You can't be laid off. So what, if you lied on your application, embezzled a few bucks, or threatened your boss. You're bulletproof.

If you're serious about improving your station in life, you should enroll in an upcoming training program. East Point Military Academy is now offering courses for a career as a crossing guard. If you sign up right away, you get a free beach chair to use at your post. Graduate from their six-month class and you immediately qualify for an entry-level position on a quiet street corner. If you take the one-year course, you'll come out as a full Lieutenant. As a 'Louie' you will enjoy the prestige of being saluted on the street by lower ranking crossing guards, bank security personnel and other uniformed workers. You will also make an override on the salaries of the rank and file guards that work for you, just like Amway.

If you sign up however, be prepared for a rigorous training regimen. The physical conditioning program consists of rope climbing, obstacle course maneuvers and crawling under live ammunition fire. You will also learn how to wave at passing cars without the drivers thinking that you are signaling them to turn. You'll train how to use the portable stop sign so that it always faces oncoming traffic, and where to stand so you don't get run over by a school bus. And most important, you'll learn how to unclog traffic after you've closed an intersection for a student who is still two blocks away.

The best part of a career as a crossing guard is the opportunity for advancement. Even if you start out as a Private First Grade Clunk, you can work your way up to a Six-Star KFC Colonel. And it doesn't end there. You may also be offered an opportunity to apply for a position with the union as an organizer. You can then go out and recruit other crossing guards and get an override on their salaries, just like Amway.

Golf in the Rough

Rhode Island may be the home of the Tennis Hall of Fame, but golf is the game of choice. Every course, public or private is always crowded, even the nine-hole courses. Rhode Island has the highest percentage of nine-hole courses that I have ever encountered. Maybe it's because the state is so small and there isn't enough room for a lot of full-size golf courses.

As a transplant coming from another state, there are things I see that are immediately different about Rhode Island golf. The etiquette, for instance, is somewhat dissimilar than what the Ancient Order of St. Andrew envisioned.

The first time I played Triggs in Providence, I captured the gritty flavor of golf in Rhode Island. My friend Guy and I were standing on the first tee ready to hit when the next foursome pulled up to the tee, immediately behind our cart. You should understand that when there is a group on a tee, etiquette calls for the next group to stay back and not approach the tee until the first group has hit their tee shots. Not only did this foursome come right up to the tee, but the driver of the first cart was berating his passenger loud enough for the group in front of us, out near the green, to hear every word. And the words were interesting. 'I don't pay you to fucking think. I do the fucking thinking and you do the fucking doing.' Our colorful golfer also wore clothes to match his speech. He sported a white silk sports shirt embellished with red and black martini glasses. The open collar featured about a pound of gold chains with the requisite evil-protecting horn. If he weren't wearing a black straw hat with a red hatband, you would think he was dressed for a nightclub date. And as with all Rhode Islanders, he was over-the-top friendly. Just when Guy was in the top of his backswing, He yelled to us, 'Hey, how you guys doin?'

Compared to other states, golf at public courses in Rhode Island plays slow. I mean really slow, like the speed of a melting glacier. A typical round takes a minimum of five hours, and one course in South County will take six hours or better on a weekend. It seems Rhode Islanders playing public courses tend to hit erratically, and will retrieve their lost ball or find twenty others, whichever comes first.

I don't think there's a dress code for golfers in Rhode Island. If there is, I haven't been able to break it yet. I grew up with the understanding that men played with open collared knit shirts, tucked into their pants and wore golf shoes. They never wore jeans or other clothing that you would not find sold in a golf pro shop. Not so in Rhode Island. You will encounter overalls, cargo pants, cut-off jeans, tee shirts, tank tops, sweats, work shoes, sneakers and combat boots.

Some other interesting things I've seen on Rhode Island golf courses are people walking through sand traps on their way to the next tee; golf carts being driven into the woods, or across streams in search of an errant ball, and through bunkers if they are in the way; and golfers hitting shots off paved cart paths and greens.

So if you play golf in Rhode Island, remember the number one rule of golf, 'Keep your head down'. Anything else will be too distracting. Oh, and bring lots of food. You may miss a meal while you're out playing in the tall grass.

Size Does Matter

Whenever I travel around the country to give a seminar or make a presentation, I find that people have no concept of the size of Rhode Island. For instance, they can't believe that in the entire state there is only one NBC television station, while other states may have five to ten, depending on how many metropolitan areas their state has. So when describing Rhode Island, I say it's about the size of an Australian sheep farm. Of course, most people don't know how big a sheep farm is, so they still don't get it. All they can visualize is sheep manure stretched from here to the horizon. I've since found out that the King Ranch in Corpus Christie, Texas is about the size of Rhode Island. Think about how your butt would feel after riding that range.

While I have trouble describing the size of Rhode Island, other people use Rhode Island's size to depict other areas. Last year's massive wildfires in Southern California burned an area that TV journalists described as about the size of Rhode Island. A sports announcer once called the strike zone of a tall baseball player, bigger than Rhode Island. The ice shelf that broke off the coast of Antarctica last year was described as the size of Rhode Island. The Golan Heights is a region a little smaller than Rhode Island.

Rhode Island comprises 1,545 square miles including Narragansett Bay, which itself is 500 square miles. Still confused? Think of it as the size of Yosemite National Park or The National Marine Sanctuary off the coast of Massachusetts.

While most Americans think of Rhode Island as small, Rhode Islanders think of their state as large. Some people in Woonsocket don't even know where Providence is. People living in the West Bay area are reluctant to travel across the bridge to East Bay because it's too far away. How small can a state be if it can have two license plates that both have the number one? And Rhode Islanders, in order to increase the perception of the state's size, nicknamed their state, The Ocean State. Of course, I can't think of an ocean on the planet that's as small as Rhode Island. There are lots of lakes that are bigger than Rhode Island.

Electing the President

Democratic Presidential candidate John Kerry claims that the leaders of the most influential countries around the world want him to be the next president. I found that statement as fascinating as are most of Kerry's comments. They always seem to contradict his previous statement on any given topic. I decided to do a little investigative journalism and find out what's the real deal.

I called the Mariachi of Caribbe in Latin America. His country boasts the world's only commercially farmed herds of wild faux. Through extensive stem cell research and cloning, the tiny nation, half the size of Staten Island, produces 90% of the world's faux suede in all of the most popular colors. The Mariachi's press secretary, Zophtic Mehlons, who is also one of his twelve wives, confirmed that His Dictatorship was indeed supporting Kerry. During the course of the conversation, however, she did let it slip that the candidate's wife, Teresa Heinsite had promised if The Mariachi blessed the candidacy, she would re-decorate at least six of their homes around the world in faux suede. The problem was that Kerry kept changing his mind about the colors. Lady Zophtic assured me that if El Mariachi didn't deliver, she would have his hide.

I then called Prince Bugabututu in the primitive African nation of Deehpdung. Frankly, given the ravages of that war-torn country, I was surprised to reach His Warlordship. But he answered the phone himself at his summer hut in Shawltown. Bugabututu confirmed that Kerry was his man. In fact, he spoke to Kerry right after the Botox injections, commenting that John had trouble pronouncing his name. It seems that the facial work left him swollen and unable to smile. In return for

41

Bugabututu's endorsement, Kerry promised to petition the UN and get more peacekeepers sent to Deehpdung. The Prince went on to say that he was pleased that Kerry was recommending these elite UN troops, as the last batch were delicious.

On the other side of the ballot, President George Doubleya asks the question, 'So who does Osama bin Laden want to be the next president?' He goes on to say, 'Then that's the candidate you should not vote for.' This sent me scurrying off to find Osama and put the question to him. It took quite an effort, but I found Osama sitting with French President Jock Shiercrappe at a coffee shop in Athens during the Olympics. In shock, I asked, 'Osama, what are you doing there in Athens?' He said, 'With all this security, there's no safer place in the world right now.' I then put the big question to him and he replied, 'I'm voting for Ralph Nader. He will ensure that the weapons reviews in Consumer Reports will be accurate.'

I then turned and asked Le Jock who he preferred, and he said, 'I support Monsieur Kerry. First, he looks French. And wiz zee Cowboy Administration's embargo against zee French, we so flooded wiz wine zat we're washing our Citroens wiz it. And besides, Le Bushie ees killing my investments in Iraq. He cancelled zee Oil for Bleu Cheese Programme.'

So there you have it. Osama wants Nader, and all the respected leaders of the world, including some of our closest 'allies' want Kerry. No doubt it's going to be a close race, and most of us are confused by our emotions. However, with Bush, you know what you can expect. With Kerry, what you think you have today will change tomorrow.

All About Florida

    With the kind of winter taking place in New England, you're probably thinking about a Florida vacation. If you're going to make the trek to the Sunshine State, then you should know a little about it. First you should understand that there are no native Floridians here. Everyone in the state is a transplant. Of course, there were Florida natives a long time ago, Seminoles, Crackers, Yahoos and such. But between the alligators and the mosquitoes, they've all become extinct. So more recently in the history of Florida, people came down from Boston and New York, saw all the beautiful high-rises in places like Miami and moved in. And that's how the state was populated. Then they started renting condos in the winter to New Englanders. And that's how the Snowbird species emerged.

    Now let me tell you about the people that do live here. Most of them are really old. I guess that's why they refer to Florida as God's waiting room. Everything here is focused on the seniors. The radio stations don't play oldies. They play music that is older than dirt. Where else can you hear Bing Crosby's father sing?

    Everyone drives a big-ass Cadillac. It's seems that they are the only cars sold in Florida, and they're special models. They're bigger than a limousine and I don't think they have a front seat. The drivers must sit on the floor, as you can never see them over the steering wheel. These cars always travel at 15 mph even though they always drive in the passing lanes on the Interstate. On those rare occasions when they hit passing gear they accelerate up to 25 mph. Most of the time they do this to restart their heart. Their cars either come equipped with no turn signals, or they have one that's always on. These people live miraculous lives in their big cahunas. They never have a car accident. It always happens just behind them. When they're not driving their Caddys, they're tooling around the neighborhood in their custom golf carts, which look just like their cars: fins, chrome and all. Traffic lights stay red for at least eight minutes, and drivers use the time to take their afternoon naps.

Restaurants have their early-bird specials starting at 4 pm The dining rooms are empty by six and closed by eight. And unlike Rhode Island, the topography is completely flat. The highest point in the state is the Okeechobee Landfill outside of Miami.

And you thought Disney World was the only point of interest in Florida.

Utility Officials Take the Gas Pipe

Did you hear about the problem with the dredging of the Providence River? We barely averted a disaster when it was discovered that the main gas lines under the river were not as deep as reported. The giant dredging equipment would have torn up the pipes causing a catastrophic gas cloud over Providence, not unlike some previous clouds that have hung over the city (most of them emanating from the State House). Blueprints for the pipe location apparently contained conflicting data.

Project managers from the Army Corps of Engineers became suspicious when officials from the gas company provided inconsistent information on the depth of the pipes. The utility's Director of Piping asserted that he was certain that the pipes had been laid at the correct depth. And he was taking no responsibility if there was a movement in the bowels of the river. In responding to the charges from the Corps Engineers, the gas officials were fuming. They explained that the gas pipes were at the proper depth because they had been placed in the same trench under the river as all the sewerage waste lines.

Of course, everyone in Rhode Island already knows that the Providence River *is* the sewerage waste line. The Army engineers confirmed that on the night of the Superbowl. One hour after the game, the level of the water in Narragansett Bay rose up over two feet.

In describing the potentially catastrophic disaster, the head engineer from the Corps explained that the severe winter weather had caused a temperature inversion over the city, trapping greenhouse gases that normally escape into the atmosphere. (If greenhouses make that much gas, why don't they just outlaw them, or capture the gas and use it in the blimps at football games?) Had the gas pipes been ruptured by the giant clamshell excavator that was dredging the river, a tremendous amount of natural gas would have escaped from the river. This, combined with all the other natural and unnatural gases in the river, would have collided with all that hot air emanating from the Legislature over the ethics flap, and that would have created the perfect storm. The resulting explosion would have been beyond your wildest imagination. The Capital Dome would have ended up in Woonsocket, where nobody would have recognized it, as no one from there has ever been to Providence.

Relieved that a tragedy had been averted, all parties worked together to solve the problem. It seems that the pipes are deep enough in the middle of the channel, but not along the shoreline. The compromise solution called for the dredging to be shallower in the area of the pipes so as not to disturb them. Unfortunately, this creates a kind of speed bump in the river. (I'm not making this up.) I personally have never seen a speed bump on water, but if it slows boats in the no-wake zone, then I'm all for it.

Where's the Beef?

Recently a billboard advertisement was put up on Route 195 showing the Virgin Mary holding a chicken carcass under the headline 'Immaculate Conception'. The organization responsible for the sign is an animal rights group that is trying to get people to stop eating meat. The group is called PETA (People Eating Tasteless Alternatives) and is probably funded by such trade associations as Soybean Producers of America and California Bean Sprout Growers. They chose Rhode Island to deliver this disrespectful message because we have the largest percentage of Catholics of any state. I guess they wanted to insult as many people as possible with one ad. However, if that were the case, why didn't they select New York, which has the highest percentage of Jews in the country? They could have shown a picture of Moses holding a beheaded pig. I'm not really sure why they picked Catholics since most of them still don't eat meat on Friday. They would have gotten better results if they chose a religion that eats meat every day.

In addition to the billboard, PETA has been picketing the fast food restaurants, encouraging people to avoid ordering menu items containing meat. The effort seems to be working as orders for French fries are through the roof. Reacting to the drop in demand for chicken, the KFC chain has hired a food sculptor who is taking the secret recipe breading and shaping it to look like chicken legs and breasts. They're calling it WMRP (White Meat Replacement Parts). Hey, parts is parts.

Not to be outdone, MacDonald's has responded with the new Big Macless. It's two all soy patties, with special sauce, lettuce, pickles and tomatoes on a sesame seed bun. Pizza Hut has also jumped on the meatless wagon and is offering a new Pepperoni Pizza made with sliced radishes.

Just when PETA got on a roll and meat sales began plunging nationwide, women discovered the Atkins and South Beach diets. They can't seem to get enough bacon, prime ribs and lamb chops, so PETA was back to square one. In a desperation move, they created the Mad Cow scare and now everyone is afraid to eat beef. Taking it a step further, they claim that the diseased cattle are being fed to chickens, pigs and sheep. And of course, there's all that mercury in the tuna fish. It looks like we're returning to our youthful dinner horrors of spinach, broccoli and peas.

But take heart all you people who refuse to eat your veggies. There are enough roaches in New York City to feed the world for five years. Look for roach farming to become the newest cottage industry, replacing alpacas and llamas.

Dress Code

Shortly after we moved to Rhode Island from New Jersey, my wife Sara volunteered to serve on the committee for the American Cancer Society Charity Ball. We were excited about participating in this worthy cause and attending our first big social event in Newport.

The setting was magnificent, a famous mansion on the ocean, opulently decorated as though they were expecting the Vanderbilts to attend. As we wandered around the grounds looking chic in our formalwear and hobnobbing with the impeccably dressed socialites, I noticed a gentleman wearing a brown tweed, winter weight sports jacket with patched sleeves. I was appalled at his wardrobe selection, knowing that this was a formal black-tie event, and it was in the late spring. Of course, he was wearing a black tie, one of those leather-string things with a turquoise slide. If he had on jeans, his ensemble could be described as *Texas Formal.* This was my first experience with the unusual dress code in Rhode Island.

The workplace is another adventure in fashion. There's one employer where men are expected to wear only white dress shirts and preferably red ties. They can remove their suit jackets while in their own office, but must put them on to visit the men's room or any other destination in the building. One of my previous employers required shirts and ties, but you certainly didn't need to put on a jacket to get a drink of water from the fountain. Fridays were *Casual Days* and the dress code was relaxed. To me *casual* means *business casual*, slacks, knit shirts, open collars, etc. Walking the hallways at my office on Fridays you would think it was gardening day or trash removal day. People wear frayed jeans, stained tee shirts and grungy sneakers, and the

49

clothes smelled like they were due for their semi-annual washing.

This isn't to say that everyone in Rhode Island is a candidate for the Worst Dressed List. Quite the contrary, most people dress beautifully. The department stores and boutiques sell a lot of high fashion merchandise to both men and women. Although you will sometimes see a couple wearing conflicting outfits. She is dressed to be photographed for the cover of Rhode Island Magazine, and he's ready to change the oil in his car. And I don't want to sound like it's just men who have no sense of style. I've seen women, legally obese, wearing spandex tights that are so stretched out that you can see the freckles on their butt. (At least I think they're freckles.) Or a gal with thighs like a middle linebacker, wearing a micro mini-skirt. What happened to covering those flaws that we all have?

Now, when Sara asks me what's the dress regimen for a particular event we're attending, I say, 'It's Rhode Island. Wear anything you want.'

Providence Tea Party

In an effort to solve the chronic budget problems in Rhode Island, the governor came up with a truly revolutionary idea. Taking a page from his counterpart in Oregon, His Governorship announced that there would be a tax on luxury blends of coffee. In this way, the tax would be borne by the rich who prefer specialty coffees, and not by the working class, who like their brew cheap, black and bitter. Although the governor tried to keep the tax plan a secret, someone spilled the beans to the press and they ran the headline 'Governor Plans to Spike Your Coffee.' The tip came from an anonymous source in the opposition party. When confronted, the unidentified Republican defended himself saying, 'There no (coffee) stains on this jacket.'

Well the people of Rhode Island also had a revolutionary idea. 'Let's dump the coffee beans in the bay and show the governor what we think of his tax' cried one vocal opponent. 'Whoa!' responded the fishermen. 'We can't have the fish up all night. They'll be too tired and fidgety to get caught the next day.' The director of *Save the Bay* weighed in and noted that if the bay turned brown from the coffee, they wouldn't be able to monitor all that other pollution coming out of Providence. Reaction from Federal Hill was particularly strong. One café owner warned, 'Nobody's a gonna add nuthin' to my cappuccino, except maybe a little Grappa.'

But the governor stood his grounds, and he stated that this was a painless tax, just like the 'sin taxes'. (For those of you not acquainted with this use of political vernacular, so-called sin taxes are levies on tobacco, alcohol, gambling, etc. I've always felt that if politicians could figure out how to collect them, there would be taxes on the other sins, such as infidelity, coveting and missing Mass on Sundays.)

The governor's plan called for a progressive tax (what's progressive about any tax?) where the tax would increase with each item added to the brew. For example, black coffee is not taxed, but if you add one sugar, it's taxed 1%, two sugars, 2% (artificial sweeteners would be double). Skim milk adds 1%, Half & Half, 2%, latte 3% (What is latte, anyway? What kind of a cow does it come from?). The governor would not accept compromise on this bill. He said, 'The last thing I want is a watered-down coffee bill.'

The bean counters in the tax department are still working out a table of charges for the exotic blends. So don't even think about ordering Extra Dark Sumac Scented Deciduous Blend with Infused Banyan Sap, or Madagascar Mocha Cannelloni Bean with Shaved Daikon Root and Steamed Caribou Milk. And what about those Crapaccino drinks? You can be sure that they will cost you at least a buck just in taxes.

Another idea percolating in the governor's mind is taxing your home brew. Can you imagine being stopped by the caffeine police on your way to work to check out your thermos? I bet that will leave a bitter taste in your mouth.

If you're concerned that your favorite blend will be taxed out of existence, you'd better move quickly. This legislation is on a fast track, so contact your legislator right away, preferably by Espresso Mail. Remember, if coffee goes down, can doughnuts be far behind?

HAPPI Demonstrators at City Hall

As if Mayor Cicillini didn't have enough on his mind, he's now facing a protest march organized by the trade group HAPPI (Hairpiece Association of Providence Plantations, Inc.). In fact, it's what's on the mayor's mind (or not) that has caused the furor.

It seems that the new mayor, unlike his predecessor is choosing to wear his own hair au naturale in public. This is causing a serious decline in popularity of hairpieces. According to Matt Weaver, president of HAPPI, business is falling off like so many follicles in the shower drain. Says Weaver, 'As the mayor of the Renaissance City, His Honor must set the example, much like the previous mayor did. Back then, business was booming! Why I could name dozens of prominent Rhode Islanders who wore their crown supplements with pride. He's setting a dangerous precedent by revealing a shameful amount of (forehead) flesh in public.'

Cicillini, at an impromptu press conference, defended his record, denying the allegations by this special interest group, 'I ran on a pro-choice platform. I have enough of my own hair and I wear it natural, not pasted down like some TV personalities. And I don't need makeup to prevent annoying reflection from camera lights.' He pointed out that he likes to dress with his shirts open with at least three buttons undone, revealing a tasteful amount of pectoral hair. Under interrogation from the press, however, he admitted that he blow-dries his chest, and that he uses Rogaine Cream on his knuckles, arms and back.

Regrouping after the failed attempt to convert the mayor, Matt Weaver and his faux-follicled members are resorting to their back-up plans. They are introducing a synthetic product to replace divots on golf course fairways. And still in development is a Kevlar-reinforced hairpiece that doubles as a bicycle helmet.

The mayor meanwhile, is rumored to be shopping for a new hat.

The Real Poop
On the Dog Track

Have you heard the scuttlebutt on the dog track? Well some people call it scuttlebutt, but really, it's just dog excrement. This has all come about over the cuts being made in the budget, but I'm jumping ahead.

Last year, when the new governor took office, he vowed to make good on his campaign promise to end the subsidies paid to the dog track owners. As he moves to pull the plug on this $10 million handout, the owners of this incredibly profitable landmark are taking steps to absorb the hit. After all, they don't want to start driving their own limousines. They have begun cost-cutting measures that would reduce staff and trim overhead. This has the unions up in arms and the track's vendors worried over the loss in business.

One of the hardest hit vendors will be The Capital Grill. They are still reeling from the scare a few weeks ago. I'm sure you read the article in the papers about the female patron who, after a few too many Dirty Martinis, looked in the glass meat case next to the bar and screamed, 'That beef is covered with Mad Cow Disease!' The place cleared out in a matter of minutes, and it hasn't been the same since. And now the track is canceling its rather substantial weekly order of aged prime Black Angus beef. The track owners haven't told the dogs yet, but they're being switched to canned dog food. And on the track, the dogs are now running even faster, as they would rather eat a mechanical rabbit than Alpo.

The lobbyist for the dog track, a prestigious law firm connected to the Legislature has been advising the owners on these cost-saving measures. In an effort to protect their own seven-figure fees, they have also suggested cutting back on the expensive union labor and hiring illegal aliens to clean up after the dogs. After all, these foreigners will soon have all the benefits of citizenship.

The union responded that they wouldn't take a workforce reduction standing up, so they staged a work slowdown where they only walked the dogs once every other day. Well you can imagine the discomfort of the dogs not being able to go regularly. When the slowdown didn't work, they did a sit-in on the track. Unfortunately some of the men actually sat on the poops, and they got angry at the dogs because they had to send their uniforms out to the dry cleaner at eighteen bucks a pop. You can image how desperate the dogs must have been. Have you ever tried a bowel movement while running at 40 miles per hour?

The Kosher Nostra

Last week the Feds made an arrest of a Mafia operative who was connected with the Patriarca crime family in Rhode Island. I was surprised that the Mafia was still organized and operating in New England. I was led to believe that, using the RICO Act (which was named after crime syndicate czar Rico *Rusty Nails* Balducci) the FBI had eliminated the Mafia. Of course, as an Italian kid, I was led to believe that there was no such thing as the Mafia. It was really the product of overzealous Jewish writers in Hollywood, who were taking advantage of our colorful Italian heritage. But later we learned that there really was a Mafia. In fact, after movies like *Goodfellas, Married to the Mob*, and *Whacked in Waco*, copycat mobs were forming all around the world. This notoriety spawned the Chinese Mafia and the Russian Mafia. You probably remember the credit card scam using Russian Express credit cards. They used the slogan, 'Don't leave home.' The most notorious crime family in that country came from Siberia and they were known as Tufschitski Ohnyu. They moved in on the vodka industry and cornered the worldwide distribution. Back then a half-gallon of vodka sold for 124,000 rubles (about $3.00). Now Kettle One goes for $35 a fifth. After a while, the Russian mob was making so much money that Putin had the KGB take them over.

As dangerous as the Russian gangs were, the Chinese Mafia was easily the most frightening of them all, and probably because of all those Kung Fu movies. They started out pressing the laundry business and before you knew it, none of the Chinese hand laundries were doing their own shirts. They were sending them out to Lo Mein Starch Works, which was actually a front to launder money, not shirts. That success led them to prey on the mom and pop Chinese restaurants. They took over the food distribution selling everything from bok choy to fortune cookies. Then they created artificial shortages in order to inflate prices. You probably recall when all the cats in the neighborhood disappeared, and you couldn't buy MSG anywhere. Soon the local Chinese restaurants closed down, only to be replaced by the now popular grand buffets.

While everyone was paying attention to these well-chronicled, organized crime families, a low profile, underground kibbutz was taking hold in the Brighton Beach section of Brooklyn. You probably haven't heard of the Jewish Mafia, but they're out there. Hymie, *The Needle* Needleman has controlled the garment district in New York for years. Any clothing manufacturer that fails to pay The Needle's 'consulting fees' gets a visit from the *Goyem Goons*, who tear up every garment in sight. That's how they got the term 'Rag Trade'. And Abie, *Bagels and Lox* Lefkowitz gets protection money from every kosher deli from Miami to Boston. Now you know why the deli waiters are so cranky. But probably the biggest scam of them all cuts into the circumcision business. The Kish Meyn Tokhes mob gets a cut of every circumcision in the country, and the rabbis don't even get to keep the tips.

Two Degrees of Separation

A brilliant mathematician once determined that throughout the world we are all connected by six degrees of separation. That means that a lifeguard at Westerly Beach and a dogsled driver in Siberia are actually sixth cousins. Same thing goes for a Montana cowboy and a Liberian mine worker. How can that be?

More recently, a zoologist in Providence has determined that in Rhode Island we all have only two degrees of separation. As preposterous as that seems, it's probably true. In the few years I've lived in this state, I'm convinced that every Rhode Islander is related. There isn't a person I meet that isn't related to someone I met last week or last month. Whenever I mention someone's name, the person I'm talking to says, 'Oh yeah, he's my cousin, my Aunt Mary's oldest kid.' Or 'She's related to my sister-in-law's niece on her father's side.'

If by some odd chance two people are not directly related, then they're childhood friends. 'Are you related to Anthony Fracciacomo?

'We graduated the same year at Classic. I dated his cousin Tessie's girlfriend, Elaine.' Or 'Rosalie Fonseca and I were in Sister Mary Nun's class at St. Francis. Her sister Kathy worked with me at Caserta's Pizza on the Hill.'

Constantly hearing all this historic banter, I came to the conclusion that Rhode Island is one big happy family. I would hate to have to chart out that family tree on Ancestry.com.

One thing that is bothering me about all this, however, is marriage. If everyone's related, how do you find someone that you can legally marry? After you eliminate all your relatives, there's not much left to choose from. I also realize that Rhode Islanders must be very understanding. If everyone is related or a friend, then they all know about each other's warts, blemishes and quirks. And so, in order to marry someone that's not your relative, you've got to be accommodating beyond a shadow of doubt.

Is there a lesson to be learned from this genealogy exercise? You bet! Next time you're on the highway and someone cuts you off, don't flip them the bird. It's probably your cousin Vinnie, and he'll tell grandma.

Building Permit – An Oxymoron

Have you ever taken on a project like renovating your old house or building your dream home? For sheer terror, it easily beats Busch Gardens' 90-degree vertical plunge on its new roller coaster ride. The construction industry is a challenge at every level, but nothing beats the non-stop horror of dealing with the government bureaucracies that oversee all building and renovation projects.

Your first step in the laborious process is to get site approval. So, if you're within 30 miles of any body of water (inflatable pools qualify) you need the DEM (The Rhode Island version of the EPA with lots more teeth and much more attitude) to sign off. Here's a typical exchange.

'Sir, I see you added a non-conforming water feature to your back yard.' 'Actually, no. That's just the septic tank. It's overflowing again.'

'Yes, but the endangered, Eight-Legged Mud Snitch (Octogamus Tattlus) has made the site its new home.'

'Yea, well, we're getting sewers installed next month and that puddle will be cleaned up and re-graded.'

'Not in my lifetime.'

Of course, you're wondering if the sewers will actually be hooked up next month. The street has been laced with open horizontal and vertical trenches for nearly a year, causing you to park three blocks from home. And now that the ditches have filled with water, the county and the contractor are fighting over who will pay for the drainage, and where will they dispose of the water And of course, there's the genius that decided to bury the electric and phone lines while the sewers were being excavated. For months now, the poles have been removed and the lines have been lying on the ground, marked with yellow crime-scene tape, awaiting the new trenches to be dug. My neighbor called the utility company to get a completion date, and when told they couldn't provide one, she calmly stated, 'You might want to prioritize this. My landscaper is lying on my lawn, apparently electrocuted.' With that she hung up.

The building department will tell you that they are there for your protection, and that they are your friend. Don't believe it. For example, they will never voluntarily give you any advice or information. After you spend tens of thousands of dollars over a six-month period on surveys, architectural drawings and engineering certifications, the department dictator tells you that they changed the setbacks in your community. And now your proposed addition doesn't conform, causing you to start from scratch with a new plan that legally fits your lot.

Inspections are always the most fun, and one of the best cures for a slow heart rate. Oh, but I'm jumping ahead. When you submit your plans to the building office, do not hand over a set of drawings that have been rolled in the customary fashion. They must now be folded, and folded in a very specific sequence of left to right and top to bottom folds. When you finally get your approved plans and permit, you will receive a schedule of required inspections. This is another lie. There are required inspections that are not listed on the schedule. For instance, after you've satisfactorily completed nearly all of your inspections and you are painting the walls, the building department will notify you that you didn't complete the 'window and door frame inspection' (not on the list). You now have to open all the walls to reveal if the windows and doors are attached to the

exterior framing in compliance with the new code.
Right. They haven't told you about that new code either.

After two glorious years completing a six-month project that has now cost you $150,000 more than you budgeted, your dream house is complete.

And you've just been transferred to Kansas City.

Baseball Rules

Once again, devoted sports fans have worked themselves into a frenzy rooting for their favorite baseball team, only to be frustrated for the umpthteen time. The mighty, power-hitting Boston Red Sox, led by the best pitcher in baseball, caved in the final innings of the seventh game and lost to the hated Yankees. And all of New England is in a depression that no amount of Zoloft can reverse. And it will last until next spring, after the draft takes place, the trades are made, and training camp opens. And that's when the euphoria begins to flow again.

The rabid fans will look at next year's team of millionaire athletes, and hope will spring forth that 'This will be the year we break the curse.' I could never understand why they call them rabid fans. I've never seen one foaming at the mouth, or bite another fan. Although I have seen fans that would appear to have had their brains infected with the dread disease. Look at some of those Cubs fans that tried to get at the guy who tipped the fly ball in game six. They would have made a pit bull look like a Chia pet.

When you stop and think about it, baseball is a pretty dull game to watch. The game drones on for hours, with batters and pitchers, each taking turns stepping off the mound or out of the batter's box in an effort to get a psychological edge. And the team of announcers, pontificating whether the last pitch, which sailed 10 feet over the batter's head was a split-finger fastball or a knuckleball slider. Who cares? It was a wild pitch. And the quirky routines that the batters go through before they are ready to step up to the plate and be embarrassed by looking in a call strike three. Take Nomar Garciaparra, for instance, he has a patented series of moves where he touches the straps on each batting glove several times while balancing the bat in one hand. He then pats his forearm, sweatband and does the gloves again. This is followed by each foot going toe to heel several times before he's set in the box. Then, as the pitcher begins his wind-up, Nomar, steps out of the batter's box and does the entire routine again. His contemporary on the Yankees, Derek Jeter, does a spoof where he mimics Nomar's full complement of moves. It's so funny that it could become a stand-up comic routine for Derek in the off-season.

Well, Red Sox fans, there's always next year, or is there? In the spring, the fans will start to emerge from their hangover and begin building their hopes, only to be disappointed again. The reason I can say that with such conviction is because the Red Sox management keeps raising the ticket prices. Now you have to have a seven-figure net worth to afford decent seats at Fenway. So there really is no incentive for the Red Sox management to pull all the stops and field a World Series team. Let me explain.

Years ago, when the Giants football teams were giving New Yorkers nightmares with their multi-decade series of creative ways to lose football games, the Marra family, in an effort to quell a fan revolt, pledged that they would not raise ticket prices until they won a Superbowl. And guess what, they did, twice. Can you imagine if the Boston management had made that promise so many years ago, after the Babe Ruth thing? You could probably get bleacher seats for a nickel. Of course, the hot dogs would set you back ten bucks.

But one of these years the Red Sox are going to win the Series! And will it be worth it? I doubt it. Look at all the years of pain and suffering New Englanders have gone through, including the medication, the therapist bills, and the loss of productivity. One win isn't going to cut it. The exhilaration starts to wear off the next day. Within a week you forgot about baseball and start thinking about football. Maybe you should start rooting for the Brockton Bowling Team.

War of the Roses

When we moved here, I said to Sara, 'This is a wonderful climate to grow fruits and vegetables. Let's plant a garden.' She said, 'Why don't we plant flowers instead? We can always buy vegetables.'

Since I'm known as the Salad Bar Terrorist up and down the eastern seaboard (restaurant managers have a picture of me in their office under the caption 'Persona Non-Grated'), we planted radishes, lettuce and arugula. We also planted lots of rose bushes (Sara's favorite), flowering trees and shrubs, and a fig tree, which is traditional in both my Italian family and Sara's. Within two months, however, the vegetable garden was decimated and there were these 35 lb. rabbits running around the yard bullying the neighborhood dogs, cats and raccoons.

Then the deer showed up and discovered the flowering and vegetable foliage, in particular the fig tree. Apparently, fig trees are like Haagen Dazs to the deer. They ate the tree right down to the roots.

With the fig tree gone, we had our landscaper select and plant a new and bigger fig tree. The deer came back, and even invited their out-of-town cousins to enjoy the feast. They were also eating the other trees, bushes and plants, particularly the rose bushes that the landscaper had planted. So we went to war. We bought a bottle of the hottest, spiciest sauce known to man. It's packaged in a Kevlar flask and contains a mixture of concentrated jalapeno, habanero and chili peppers in a base of sulfuric acid. We sprinkled the sauce on the leaves of the plants. I said to Sara, 'They will come one more time, and that's it.'

Well, that wasn't it. They came back again, this time wearing bibs. And to show their appreciation, they left piles of deer pellets alongside the beds. It must be like the Chinese custom of belching in front of your host to show you enjoyed the meal. The more hot sauce we sprayed, the more deer showed up. That's when we realized that they were a strain of Mexican deer. So, we had to try another tactic. I went to the local Home Depot and was told industrial strength fermented concentrate of fox and coyote urine would do the trick. We liberally splashed that around all the trees, shrubs and flowerbeds, confident that we had won. But we then encountered an unexpected technical glitch. Every dog in the neighborhood is now peeing in our backyard, and the deer are still there.

I went back to Home Depot and told the 'Associate' what to do with his urine. He then sold me a 100 ft. roll of chicken wire fencing and advised me to buy a pair of rawhide gloves. Oh, what fun I had uncoiling the fencing and wrapping it around the trees and shrubs. I looked like Kramer at the end of the Seinfeld Cock Fight episode.

Well, it actually worked. The deer can't get at the vegetation, but all the chickens in the neighborhood have moved inside the fencing. And now I have all these eggs, but my friends and neighbors are all on cholesterol medication.

EGads.com

As consumers get more comfortable with the Internet, they are taking advantage of more and more services and features of this revolutionary and evolving communications tool. One of the categories that is experiencing a meteoric rise in popularity is computer dating. With the tremendous power of the 'net to collect data, there's not much you can't find out about a prospective mate. Computer dating services build huge files of people who are looking to meet other people without going through a painful exploratory dating ritual. But just how accurate are those files? And how well do these services work?

I spoke to some of my single friends and asked about their experiences. My nephew paid $3,000 for a membership in an executive dating service that guaranteed up to 300 dates. At $10 a lead, this sounds like a bargain. But if you're not looking to break the Guinness Book of Records for dating, selecting a life partner from 300 candidates can be a mind-numbing exercise. Just scrolling through hundreds of files of prospects to find the right 'specifications' for your date must be extremely difficult. How do you really know what you want in a mate? Do you take the time to write a job description?

And the way people exaggerate their qualities, 300 prospects may not be enough. People lie about their height, weight, measurements (I'm five feet, six. I measure 38-26-38, and I weigh 110 pounds.) Yea, right. They lie about their jobs, their salaries, number of times married, and whether they are presently married. And of course, they all like everything, until you start dating them. Then they get really selective.

There are always photos included in the files. (If there aren't, you should immediately reject them.) But what you see is not necessarily what you get. With image-enhancing retouching programs like Photoshop, you can perform the equivalent of plastic surgery in photography. Sara's friend dated a guy whose digital photo showed a good looking, muscular buff hunk. Disappointingly, a wimp that looked like he got hit by a bus showed up. And one of my friends dated what he thought was an attractive brunette. When they met, to his relief, she matched the photo. A couple of dates later, when they got intimate, she removed her clothes and wig and revealed a body completely devoid of hair. Of course, that fact was not mentioned in her file.

While I feel my friends' pain, I also recognize that they are no prizes either, with their own warts and hairy moles. And what kind of lies are they telling in their profiles? How do you overcome this inevitable disappointment? In thinking about it, I came up with a solution. Why not have a rating system, just like e-Bay? After you date someone, you complete a questionnaire, and those answers become part of the person's file. This way you can tell the pretenders from the real deal. And just maybe, computer-dating services will become part of the mainstream social process.

Meanwhile, the liquor companies and tavern owners' associations are desperately hoping this computer dating thing bombs and fades into the sunset. If it does catch on, and with smoking banned almost everywhere, there will be no reason to ever go to a bar.

Deer in the Headlights

     I read recently that the Rhode Island General Assembly has been making payments on claims from people whose cars have been damaged by deer. In fact, the trigger-happy lawmakers are even paying repair bills for fender benders that occur in parking lots if caused by a deer. And the number of these collisions has increased dramatically over the last couple of years, straining the already venison-laden budget. The governor is outraged by what he perceives as a handout to Democratic voters in need of auto body repairs.

     But the issue goes much deeper than that. It's true, the deer population has mushroomed out of control (although it has not been verified that they now outnumber Italians in the state) and the animals wreak havoc everywhere. The governor's solution is simple. Change the hunting rules, and allow open season all year long. We'd soon have the deer population under control.

     The key obstacle to this plan is a group called SMASH (Sober Moms Against Shooting the Herd). They have advocated on behalf of these beautiful, agile creatures. In fact, they previously lobbied for the bill that funded the training of deer to cross highways only at the deer crossing signs. And this is at the heart of the issue in question. The General Assembly feels because they have spent so much money erecting signs and training the deer, that they have an obligation to pay damages when one of their charges comes charging out and collides with an automobile. This is particularly true if the deer did not cross at a designated cross-leap.

     Seeing an opportunity to swell their ranks, the unions hoofed it down to the statehouse to press for a bill to require 24-hour, union crossing guards at the busiest deer crossings. Of course, these crossing guards would receive the same benefits as the school crossing guards in Cranston. And of course, they were insisting that the State pay for their training, uniforms, and full benefits packages.

But before we get too far afield, we first wanted to examine the reasons why this problem has become so exacerbated recently. The root cause can be traced back to a story that appeared in the press a while back called, 'War of the Roses'. In that article, the author described effective ways to keep deer from ravaging gardens and shrub beds. Apparently, the solutions were so effective that the deer population's feeding habitat was severely reduced. This forced them out of the suburbs, and back into the forests to forage for their meals. Instead of expensive tulip, lily and other flower buds, the deer were relegated to browse on thistle. Ugh! This gradually caused a change in the attitude of the usually docile, playful deer.

After becoming downtrodden, the deer discussed their plight with some Mideast cousins. One was a camel that had entered the country illegally to study Mad Dromedary Disease at the university. Another was an escaped goat that had been the companion of a radical cleric.

As a result, some of the angry young bucks began forming underground sleeper groups, loosely aligned with the international terrorist organization, Al Klunker. (Of course, it's hard to picture how any of these bucks could possibly do anything underground with those big bulky antlers.) But when the high holy stags told them of the rewards of martyrdom, they signed on in herds. Now, these horny young bucks are looking for opportunities to throw themselves in front of cars so they can go directly to deer heaven, claim their 26 virgins and buck the hell out of them. Before long, you can expect to see some of these bucks entering crowded malls, train stations and airports, strapped with suicide vests that are packed with explosives and filled with deer pellets.

Rubbing it In

The recent scandal in the news regarding professional baseball players using banned steroids is upsetting to everyone who follows 'America's Pastime'. Of course, we are all aware that taking performance-enhancing drugs is illegal. In fact, it's downright unsafe. Several professional athletes have died from the effects of prolonged steroid use.

I happened to find one interesting nugget is all this rhetoric about who knew what, and who took which drugs. Retired baseball star Barry Bonds claimed that he never took steroids. However, he admitted to using a special massage cream that relieved all his aches and pains. It seems though, that this magic elixir also improved his strength. Since this cream was obviously a legal substance (otherwise Barry would never have used it and risked being stripped of all those records), I decided that I wanted to try this cream out myself.

So I went on the Internet, where you can buy just about anything. I found this site that allows you to bet on football, view pictures of naked people, and buy discount Viagra. And sure enough, they had Popeye's Mother's Secret Muscle Cream.

When I got the delivery, in a plain brown wrapper, I was really excited, but a little uneasy at the same time. I decided to try the cream out on someone else first. When I asked Sara if she had any body parts that she wanted to strengthen or enlarge, she gave me a look that convinced me to never ask her that question again.

Looking for an unsuspecting candidate I spotted my neighbor's dog, a tiny Yorkie that fits in the palm of your hand. (In fact, I'm not sure they really are dogs.) I walked over and rubbed a little cream on him and when I let him off the leash, he took off and chased a pit bull into a lake full of alligators. 'Wow,' I said. 'This shit really works.'

So I began to wonder. Did the Red Sox use this muscle cream to win the World Series? Could there be any other explanation? How about the Patriots? And what would happen if the Republicans in Chicago started using Popeye's Mother's Secret Muscle Cream?

It was now the moment of truth. I had to use this magic elixir on my own body. First, I rubbed some on my scalp and within a week more hair started growing. And it was thicker, too. I began using it on my upper body and I could hit a golf ball across Narragansett Bay. And because so much of the cream came in contact with my hands, I found that I could type much faster than ever. I wrote this story in three minutes and nearly broke the keyboard.

But then something strange happened. I was playing golf and hit my drive over the green and into the bushes on the other side. When I went to retrieve my ball, I disturbed a bee's nest and was attacked by hundreds of angry worker bees. When it was over, I could barely get up and I didn't have the strength to get back in the golf cart. Then my body began to wither and shrink, and now I can't perform the simplest task without help. Sara has to dress me and spoon-feed me my Pablum in the morning. And the bees on the golf course are now the size of blue jays, and are attacking everything in sight.

The Hans is Quicker
Than the Eye

While on vacation, I arranged to meet my friends Bill Prendergast and Weaver Lindsay for dinner at Tuscany Restaurant in Westwood, NJ. When I got there, I found Bill at the bar, engaged in conversation with a very distinguished businessman who had success leaking out of his eyes. This person of interest turned out to be H. Alexander Engle, Esq. (Hans) who, as he explained, leads a firm of 300 attorneys in offices across the country and around the world. His clients include the royal family of Kuwait, and Koffi Annan's (Oil for Food scandal) son, among other notables. Our new best friend is also multi-lingual and well versed on just about any topic we introduced (politics, religion, oil, Islam, Israel, the Koran, the Bible, etc.). He quickly ordered drinks for all of us, as Weaver arrived shortly after I did. As it turns out, not only is Hans an expert skier (his Jewish father was born in Austria) but he is also a member of the ultra-exclusive Ridgewood Country Club, home of the Barclay's PGA tournament. And he quickly invited the three of us to join his private outing at Ridgewood in late August. When I explained that by then I would be back in Rhode Island, Hans touched my arm and assured me that it would not be a problem. His private jet would pick me up at Green Airport and fly me to Teterboro where his limo would take me to Ridgewood for the event.

After a few more drinks, we exchanged business cards and invited Hans to join us for dinner, but he declined, explaining that a private car was picking him up at his home in Saddle River to take him to New York City for a late dinner engagement. Hans then got a call on his cell phone and walked to the front of the restaurant to speak to his caller. He was having trouble with the reception, so he used the restaurant phone at the host station to return the call. (He had previously explained to us that he was a personal friend of the restaurant owner.) While he was on the phone, Bill paid our drink tab and we went to our table.

As soon as we sat down, I said to Bill, 'Do you know who Hans really is?' 'No. Who?' 'He's the guy who emailed me from Nigeria about his family that lost $35 million, and if I send him $5,000 he would split the thirty-five mil with me.' When we stopped laughing, the barmaid came to our table, obviously distraught. She explained that she inadvertently charged us for all the drinks and Hans had left without paying anything. I told her not to worry, as it was worth the cost of the drinks for the entertainment he provided.

We each ordered a glass of wine and some food, and then Hans magically reappeared. He apologized profusely for the confusion with the bar tab, and to make up for it, he produced a bottle of wine and placed it on the table. He again said good night and left the building.

The waiter came to the table and advised us that there would be a corkage fee to open the bottle. Recognizing that this was an expensive bottle of Chianti ($149 as we later learned), I told Bill to take the bottle home and share it with his wife. We were already well passed the legal limit, plus I was definitely having motor control issues. And we still had three full glasses on the table. Bill disagreed. 'For the ten bucks corkage fee, let's drink this wine, even if we throw out the stuff in our glasses.' Well of course, we didn't discard anything. We drank all the wine including the entire contents of the bottle. But as you guessed, the story doesn't end there.

After we finished the bottle, the waiter came to the table and anxiously explained to us that the Chianti was taken from their wine cabinet next to the host station, obviously without authorization. We would have to pay for it of course. But not to worry, the owner would not be pressing charges for the theft. He was certain that the surveillance camera would show that we did not pilfer the wine, but instead it would reveal the hands of Hans reaching into the case.

We paid our bill and staggered out of the place. And all I could think was God, I hope Weaver doesn't show up on that video tape.

Car Dealer Insider Trading

I recently made a visit to the Claude Butz Auto Mall, hoping for once that I was going to actually enjoy the car buying experience. A gorgeous blonde greeted me at the door showing so much cleavage that I thought I stumbled into a breast augmentation clinic. After the brief, one-sided conversation, I began to accept the premise of all those blonde jokes. She introduced me to my personal sales consultant, named "Slick" who leaves oil stains on everything he touches. Slick immediately became my new best friend and he was going to make it happen for me, including his employee pricing. He asked all the usual questions. 'How much do you want to spend a month?' 'How much can you put down?' 'Do you have a trade?' 'What do you think of the blonde?'

Since I did my homework on the Internet, I knew the dealer cost of the model and the options I wanted. After the usual negotiating I stood my ground, so Slick took my offer into the sales manager's office to get him to OK what he claimed was a money-losing deal. Slick came back dejected and we negotiated some more. When he returned from the third trip to the boss's office, he had the best deal he could make. If I paid cash for the floor mats, he could put me in the car of my dreams for the monthly payment that I demanded. I was ecstatic. For an extra $150 I got my deal.

But then came the handoff. Slick now brought me into the private office of the finance officer, who would 'take care of the paperwork.' When Slick closed the door behind him, I sensed that it was locked. Mr. Stikituem, previously the car dealer's leading sales rep, explained that no responsible parent would ever send a child off to school without shoes, and likewise he didn't want my new car to leave the showroom without the proper protections. Now that I'm part of the family with the employee pricing, he was putting together a special package of services for me. These included GAP insurance, extended warranty coverage, creditor life insurance, mud and salt paint protection, On Star navigation fees, hazardous spill cleanup rider, satellite radio membership, lifetime maintenance package, endangered species collision protection, and emissions control recovery fees. And the good news was that by extending my contract for only two more years, my payments would remain the same.

And then he brought me in to meet Mr. Gutrench, the service manager, who was able to immediately schedule my pre-flight burn-in, the road preparation procedure, and the 'buttons and knobs' orientation. Of course, you know don't you, that he's also on commission.

Well, when I got home from the dealership wearing nothing but my tighty-whities and desperately needing a shower with industrial-strength detergent, I read the contract. It seems that because of my excellent credit, the dealer was able to get a below market promotional loan rate (with him making a couple of points) that enabled him to sell me the car for *list price* with my negotiated monthly payment. So I cancelled the order, and I called my friend Billy from Detroit. He got me an unbelievable deal on an almost new model. Once they wash off the mud and provide a set of complimentary windshield wipers, the luxury SUV will be shipped in from Houston next week.

Law and Order
In America

When the early settlers came to America, one of their goals was to establish their own laws. And with laws, you need lawyers. Back then lawyering, or loitering as it was called, was a primitive and crude profession, much as it is today. Originally, anyone with a set of Martindale and Hubbell books could become a lawyer. But after Harvard Law School was established, things changed. As soon as the school opened its doors, The Massachusetts Tavern opened directly across the street. The first law students became lawyers if they knew the location of the tavern and could walk by it after an all-night frat-house drinking binge. They therefore 'passed the bar'. Later when temperance came into vogue, the tavern became a private club. You then had to be 'a member of the Massachusetts bar' in order to practice law. In fact, back then all you could do was practice law, as there were no courts where you could do any actual lawyering.

At some point around the turn of the century, with increasing demand for more transportation vehicles, wagon factories began to spring up. And right behind that were unions to protect the working class. With the unions demanding higher wages and shorter hours, the factory owners had to cut costs, resulting in flimsier wagons. For example, they switched to pine bumpers instead of costlier maple. After complaints about safety started rolling in, Continental Blather System (CBS) ran an episode showing a burning wagon after it was rear-ended. The wagon makers then had to fight off a government recall by lobbying their Continental Congress representatives. And so the stage was set for a major catastrophe. One foggy morning during rush hour on the Boston Post Road, there was a 20-wagon pileup. Since there were no vehicle safety standards, the one-mph impact caused extensive damage and injuries. Almost immediately, the ambulatory wagon chasers showed up and saw a bonanza. There were literally dozens of wagon makers to sue, but Nathaniel Scharque, a partner with Lute, Robb & Steele said, 'Why stop there. Let's sue all the working-class stiffs that made these wagons.' This was the first recorded class action suit. And it launched a whole new specialty in the legal profession: Tort (short for torture) Law. No more boring contracts and incorporations, now lawyers had a way to make some serious money.

Doctors were sued if their leeches sucked too much blood from a patient (an interesting analogy). George Washington sued his dentist, claiming his wooden implants had caused cancer in his gums. A female customer sued the Dunkin Scones chain for damages when she spilled hot tea in her lap while driving her buggy on a bumpy road. And Smith & Western was sued by a highway robber, because one of his S&W muskets jammed when it was used in a highway robbery. And thus began this huge transfer of wealth. Everyone with deep pockets was giving up their hard-earned money to people making frivolous claims against them. But most of the money was going to the lawyers, who justified their actions in the name of consumer protection. The lawyers, however, were smart enough to use some of the money productively. They founded the ACLU, Consumers Union, Sierra Club and the US Congress. And suddenly, everything began to cost twice as much. Tri-cornered hats, powdered wigs and breeches were priced out of existence. And the mid-wife profession became totally unaffordable as medical malpractice insurance rates soared.

And then one day, a church-going gentleman from Providence decided to get divorced. He was about to seek help from his minister, but on his way, he encountered a lawyer on the avenue. And from that moment on, for men all over the world, life has irrevocably changed.

Made in the USA
Columbia, SC
09 February 2018